THE FOUR DEPORTATIONS OF JEAN MARSEILLE

McSWEENEY'S
SAN FRANCISCO

McSweeney's and colophon are registered
trademarks of McSweeney's, a nonprofit
publisher based in San Francisco.

COVER ILLUSTRATION BY Anders Nilsen.

ISBN: 978-1-96327-013-6

10   9   8   7   6   5   4   3   2   1

www.mcsweeneys.net

Printed in the United States.

THE FOUR DEPORTATIONS *of* JEAN MARSEILLE

by

JEAN MARSEILLE

edited by LAURA LAMPTON SCOTT
and PETER ORNER

McSWEENEY'S
SAN FRANCISCO

JEAN: AN INTRODUCTION

I.

Jean Marseille was born in the Bahamas to Haitian parents during what his mother and father thought was only a brief stop. This was in 1971, during the waning days of Papa Doc Duvalier's dictatorship. As Jean once put it to me, "At that time, the Tonton Macoute"—Duvalier's vast network of henchmen—"would kill you for anything."

When Jean's parents, like so many others, decided to risk their lives in search of something—anything—different, they managed to scrounge up enough money to buy passage to the Bahamas. The plan was for the two of them to proceed to the US from there. But the baby, Jean, came early and scuttled his parents' plans. After six months or so, Jean's mother sailed for Florida, leaving Jean's father with the infant in the Bahamas. His father, in turn, packed Jean up in a cardboard box and hired a woman to carry him to Haiti (and to Jean's maternal grandparents) on a boat. Whenever Jean tells this story, and it is one he tells often, he includes the detail that his father fixed up a little bed for him in the cardboard box. Jean calls this journey from the Bahamas back to Haiti his first deportation.

Yet he remembers his childhood on his grandparents' farm outside Cap Haitien, a city on the north coast of Haiti, as a happy one. There were cows and goats and donkeys and miles to roam. His grandmother was especially affectionate. "She super-loved me," Jean says. Still, he missed the mother he'd never known. From Florida, his mother would send him cassette tapes.

The first time I heard my mother's voice was on those tapes. Think about it. Your mother's voice comes in the mail. That's my life.

When he was twelve, his mother sent for him (by then his parents had split up) by paying a couple to pose as his parents and smuggle him into the US—his second deportation, this one from Haiti to Florida. Jean spent the next eleven years in Florida, where he became an American. But things were never easy. In school, kids made fun of him for his English. Jean says he got his ass kicked more than a few times. When he was fifteen or so, Jean got into drugs, both buying and selling. He wanted girlfriends. He wanted to be cool.

You could make good money selling. I had other jobs, putting people's groceries in bags and stocking shelves, but that's $3.25 an hour at minimum wage. I was tired. I had to go to school. I'd get to work at 3:00 a.m.... The first time I sold I made $400. Some-times, in a day, I could make $600 or $700. Then I didn't get beat up so easily.

The drugs led to arrests and two serious charges: for conspiracy to distribute drugs within a thousand feet of a school, and, as he tells it, "for throwing a brick, a 'deadly missile,' they call it in the law, at a moving car." The driver, he says, was trying to run him over.

He'd been living the high life, buying cars, beating charges, but always knew it wasn't going to last. What he didn't expect was an immigration hold. Jean says, "I thought I was an American." And he was. Also, he had a green card. His understanding was that at the time, under US law, if you had a green card, you couldn't be deported.

> I always tell whites from the US that I meet, "You know who my favorite president is? Ronald Reagan." And they can't believe it. "Why do you like Ronald Reagan, man? He was a terrible president." Not for us! Haitians in the United States love Ronald Reagan. He made it clear: If you'd been in the US for over five years, you could have a green card. They would not deport you. I got my green card with the help of Ronald Reagan.

Prison, sure, possibly, but not deportation. Yet under Bill Clinton, things changed.

Clinton's deportation law hit me like a rock. It turned out you could be deported if you had a green card. If your crime was bad enough.

After several months in a federal detention center in Louisiana, Jean was flown back to Haiti, shackled to his seat on the plane—his third deportation, this time courtesy of Bill Clinton. His grandparents had long since died. There was no farm anymore. Aside from distant relatives, he knew nobody. When he got off the plane, Jean says, there were bodies on the tarmac, presumably political opponents of the regime, who'd been shot by the Haitian military.

There will always be more of Jean's story to tell. How Jean—who barely spoke Kreyòl—created a life for himself in Port-au-Prince. How he met (or rather re-met) a childhood sweetheart, the woman who would become his wife. How he became a loving father to four girls and three boys (five of his own, a stepchild, and his wife's sister's child, orphaned in the cholera outbreak that followed the earthquake). How, for decades, Jean hustled on the streets of Lavil to make ends meet, until the city's most recent descent into extreme violence.

And how he hustles day in and day out now that he's trying to create a new life for himself and his family in the Dominican Republic. In December of 2022, the situation in Haiti became so dangerous and unlivable that Jean was once again forced across an international border. He calls it his fourth deportation.

2.

I first met Jean in 2013. I'd come to Port-au-Prince to work on a post-earthquake book for Voice of Witness, a nonprofit publisher devoted to capturing living history through oral storytelling. It was my third book for Voice of Witness. I'd edited one on undocumented Americans and coedited another about Zimbabwe. I felt pretty confident I knew what I was doing. As is well known, Haiti, and Port-au-Prince in particular, was struck on January 12, 2010, by an apocalyptic earthquake that left more than three hundred thousand people dead. My plan was to speak to earthquake survivors about how they had managed to stay alive. Jean and his wife and children survived, in large measure because Jean was lucky enough, at that time, to own a sturdy house. It's important to note that many tens of thousands of deaths were caused less by the raw power of the quake itself than by the collapse of substandard buildings. In a sense, the devastation was man-made.

Jean met me at the airport. I remember vividly the way he looked me over, as if he immediately saw through my low-rent, swashbuckling writer act—my sunglasses, my notebook, my pen in my mouth, my digital tape recorder, my clunky camera—and understood, without my needing to say a word, that I didn't have a clue where I'd just landed. He knew I wanted to see the wreckage and the suffering up close. That I wanted, right away, to write about it, to capture it in recordings, on film. And that then, as quickly as possible, I wanted to go back home to my life in San Francisco, to my apartment, to my wife and kid.

Three years after the earthquake, Port-au-Prince was still ravaged. The majority of the capital's population was still living in tent cities, with plenty of hunger and desperation and ruin for me to explore, even right there at the airport, where hundreds of people jostled one another to get the attention of foreigners like me—a few journalists here and there, but mostly

NGO types who were scooped up by SUVs and spirited away to Pétion-Ville, the city's high-end district. And even though I had a much lower budget, at least I had a budget.

Jean, as I say, saw right through me. I would fly in and fly out. Sure, I'd worked on two earlier oral histories, but those were about subjects and places I knew something about. But I knew very little about Haiti and could not speak French, let alone Kreyòl. But in the same moment that Jean sized me up, he also understood how we might work together. He knew I had my hustle, just like he had his. As he himself says about Lavil (Kreyòl for "the city," which is what Haitians call Port-au-Prince):

> In Lavil, they're hustling. Everywhere. In every neighborhood you go, you will find people selling. Yes, everybody's selling something. That's the life in Port-au-Prince. Everybody's making commerce. You don't make much, but you make something for tomorrow.

My father was a glorified ambulance chaser in Chicago for forty-nine years. My father's favorite word, like

Jean's, was *hustle*. My father would tell me, "Look, kid, if you don't hustle, you're nowhere. Period."

And sure, yes, I had my budget, and out of that meager amount, I was going to pay Jean for his services as my fixer, driver, translator, all-around consigliere. He wasn't going to abandon me at the airport for being a dipshit with a pocketful of American cash. I could be useful, yes. But here's what's special about Jean: He was also generous to me in those first moments. He gave me the benefit of the doubt when I least deserved it. He said, "My name is Jean Marseille. I was born in the Bahamas, raised in Haiti and Florida. Three-time deportee. You can call me JP or Johnny or Johnny P or Money G—that's my internet name. I've worked with CNN, the *Los Angeles Times*, the *Miami Herald*, *Al Jazeera*." But under his words, he also conveyed, *Okay, you may well be a dipshit, but you're all right.*

The big guns of journalism, Anderson Cooper and the rest of them, had long since cleared out of Haiti, and Jean was left with the dregs, me. He and I would walk the streets and the tent camps of Port-au-Prince, interviewing people. One day we came across a guy selling ice cream. I suggested we talk to him, and so we did our thing. Jean would speak to a subject in Kreyòl, explaining that I was an American journalist interested in their post-earthquake lives, et cetera, et cetera. I'd ask questions and Jean would translate. Then he'd translate the person's answer back to me and we'd go on like that. This is what the ice cream vendor told us:

The music is what calls all the kids. People hear the music, they know it's me. They run and say they want krem, "Give me krem." I have chocolate, vanilla, mayi—that's made with grits. Not white grits: yellow grits. They're seven gouds. I've been selling ice cream for seven months. It doesn't work well. At the end of the day, I hand back the money to the distributor and he gives me back a little bit out of it. The distributor has a lot of people selling. A lot of people. He's a cop... I'm twenty-seven. I don't have money to do anything else, and don't want to be just sitting around. So I just live with the little profit. Until I can find something else. I do mason work besides this. But I don't have any special trade.

As we walked away I told Jean I thought that was pretty good, and it was. The ice cream man's story is an insight into the day-to-day, which is what I was looking for. We got into the specifics. The distributor, the cop, taking most of the money, and still the guy was hanging in there. Jean agreed, but he also said this:

Let me tell you a secret. We can go to a thousand merchants in this city. None of them is going to tell you, *My business is doing good!* Never. Especially if they're talking into a microphone. They're always going to tell you it's going bad, you know? Because they're looking for an angle. That's the hustle. The hustle is the work… The ice cream man, he's going to make it. Because he's resilient. He's used to suffering. But somebody who's going hungry for the first time, it's the most painful shit ever. Like when I first came here. I couldn't take the hunger.

Clearly, you get the idea of Jean's worldview, a view he shares with millions of people, including my late father. But again, note the generosity. The ice cream man's going to make it. He's resilient. That's Jean. His cynicism, as I see it, is only honest; it doesn't degrade. He roots for people, not against them.

After that conversation I realized something that should have been obvious from the beginning: Jean should be the one conducting interviews, talking directly to people, the people he knew so well, not acting as a middleman. And this is how it went as we worked together for the next four years—along with many other people, including coeditors Evan Lyon and Laura Lampton Scott—on the book that eventually became *Lavil: Life, Love, and Death in Port-au-Prince*. (Evan is a physician and writer who has spent years working and treating patients in Haiti, and Laura is a writer and professor in Portland, Oregon, who coedited these dispatches.) *Lavil* makes for rough reading. The stories of the survivors are honest and often shattering. At the same time, we did our best to celebrate life in the streets of a remarkable city. As life, even amid all that ruin, carried on. The last chapter is Jean narrating the story of his life up to that time. But his stamp is all over *Lavil* because much of the book consists of intimate interviews only he could have conducted. When he talks to people, Jean is fully absorbed. He listens with his brand of almost fervid curiosity. I have a photograph of him in the rubble of what used to be downtown Port-au-Prince. In it he is holding a recorder and listening to a woman who is selling dried fish on the ruins of what had been a municipal building, just across the street from what used to be the National Palace, what Haitians call the White House. Here's what she told Jean:

I am under the sun every day. Yes, dried fish is my business. Aranso, it's called. If someone wants it for G20 Haitian, you sell. If they want it for G10, you sell. For G5, even if it is one goud, you sell. You sell, you sell, you sell. It's a business that goes up, it goes down. You have to be in the street every day. I walk through the street singing, "Aranso! Aranso sel!" Normally, you make G50 a day. Sometimes you make G60. Other days it's G30. I pay the children's school. I have six kids of my own. I have another child of my little brother who is in my hands. If I have even G100 Haitian, I stretch it and send my children to school. I buy a pair of shoes on credit. My children need shoes for school. All this on a little case of dried fish. Six kids...

Jean is a gifted journalist. He may not have a degree in journalism, or any degree at all, but I've never in my life seen anybody as conversationally fearless—he'll talk to anybody about anything, at any time. Once, he struck up a long and fascinating conversation with a guy in Port-au-Prince's Grand Cemetery. The man's job: to watch over the grave of a dead general. All day long the man sits in front of the ornate tomb of one of Papa Doc's henchmen. A family member of the general's pays him a bit of pocket change each week. Jean's specialty is understanding the economics of how people get by when they have next to nothing to get by on. He understands the hustle of survival, because he lives it. And as he said, interviewees were a lot more candid with him than they ever would have been with me.

One essential thing he taught me: patience. He'd spend time with his interviewees, often hours. You talk, you talk about all kinds of things, you talk again, you stay in touch. Jean's technique sometimes involves asking, let's say, unconventional questions. Once, when one of his interviewees was talking a lot about her problems with love, and with men in particular, Jean asked,

"How do you know when a man loves a woman?" The woman answered:

> If a man is willing to help me, I'll open my heart to him. I don't like to date people just for their money. Men don't have to support me, because I always find jobs to take care of myself. I know there are some bad people out there, and I've already told you I'm not lucky in love. How do I know when a man loves a woman? I don't know. One day I'd like to know.

Since Jean and I last saw each other, in 2016, we've done our best to maintain our friendship through email and phone calls. As bad as things have been for his family, he always begins our conversations with questions about mine.

And I've kept up with his hustles. A few years back he had a bike rental business. He's sold barbecue, water, candy, cigarettes, ice cream. And when journalists come to Haiti, Jean always stands ready and able to assist with a story.

But it hasn't been easy, and as the situation in Haiti has become increasingly dangerous (it's always amazing to me that there is no rock bottom, that things can, somehow, get even worse than they already are), the challenges of Jean's already difficult life have increased a hundredfold. Since the assassination of President Jovenel Moïse in his own bedroom in July of 2021, criminal gangs have seized control of much of Port-au-Prince, and murders and kidnappings have become a daily reality.

In 2022, Jean's eight-year-old son was kidnapped and held hostage for weeks. In order to rescue him, Jean turned over the last of his inheritance from his mother to the kidnappers, a total of $7,000. Diego was beaten by the kidnappers, and suffered significant blows to the head. Jean was able to free him, thank god, but the family was left destitute. Jean managed to send Diego to relatives in Cap Haitien. Not long after, Jean's house was taken by a gang, along with many others along his street. Following the loss of the family house, Jean's wife and three other children—MacDonald, Annesamma, and Geyonce—also departed for Cap Haitien.

That summer, Jean remained behind in Port-au-Prince in order to secure passports and visas for his family to leave the country. It was during this period that Laura Lampton Scott and I began work with Jean on this new book. We asked Jean to record his thoughts directly into a phone app in hopes that his dispatches might give us, and potential readers, a better sense of life on the ground in Haiti during a time of unprecedented violence and chaos.

When he began these recordings, Jean was living with his second-oldest son, MacDonald, in Port-au-Prince, moving from house to house, and, at times, sleeping on the street.

During these recordings (and now), Jean needs money. He always needs money. Though I have always tried to do what I can to support Jean personally (and so have Laura, Evan Lyon, Jean's old friend Joe Mozingo, and many others who want to help), our connection is rooted in the fact that we both recognize and appreciate the hustle in the other. It's elemental. We're always trying to come up with the next one. And this book for McSweeney's is a new hustle—thank you, McSweeney's, for believing in Jean and the stories he has to tell—because Jean was paid for his work on it. He'll also receive royalties, should there be any, so please buy a copy for yourself, and why not for your friends and family? While Jean is a gifted storyteller, his experiences with violence and displacement are, unfortunately, all too common. In many ways, he's a lot better off than many of his fellow Haitian citizens. He was able to leave and begin to try and make a new life. Still, he longs for home, as anybody would. Jean continues, to this day, to fight for the survival of his family.

—*Peter Orner*

JEAN MARSEILLE'S FAMILY LINE

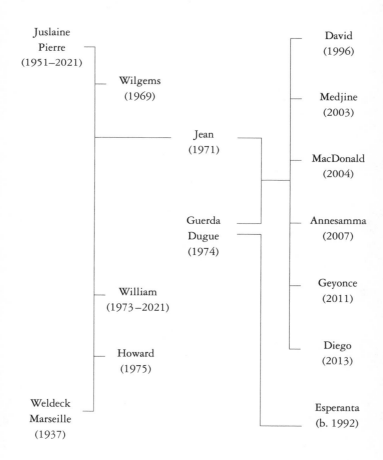

PORT-AU-PRINCE

DISPATCH: 10/18/22

This morning the sun came up, like every other day, and the violence came along with it. A lot of gunshots. You have people mostly staying inside. There's an old person that was in a house close by. Maybe he got shot, because I heard screaming. An ambulance came and took away a body. Must have been him. Right now, I'm staying in Delmas 75. I was supposed to leave today to go to another ghetto, but I wasn't able to, because of two things. One, I don't have money. Two, I owe money. I have to pay my debts before I leave. There was a big rain today, and we had to run away from the shooting through the water in the streets. When it rains in Port-au-Prince, the roads flood. When President Jovenel Moïse was assassinated, whatever work they were doing to fix up the roads, it all stopped. The roads are unpaved in this area. We have to wait a couple of days for the water to go down.

As I sit, my heart is beating really fast. I'm panicking. I just want to get out of here. The roads out of the city are still blocked and there's some war going on in Cité Soleil about the gas that's being sold on the streets for G550 ($3.77) a gallon.

There was a lot of shooting going on just now. Another group of people came through this area, just shooting.

I was deported to Haiti in 1994 for some things I did back in the day in the United States. I don't want to talk about it. I've talked about it enough.

It's always been hard for me in Haiti as a deportee. Hard to get work. People don't always trust deportees. They wonder what you did to get kicked out of the United States. Ever since I came to Port-au-Prince, the only way I've been staying alive is through the international community. When reporters or people who work for NGOs come to Haiti, I get some work, as a driver, fixer, translator—I help out in all kinds of ways. Even after they leave, a lot of these internationals keep me in mind and help me and my family out a little. I used to do a lot of work with a woman from the *Miami Herald*. Lately I got in contact with her and she's been saving me. Otherwise, I might already be dead.

Money is always a problem. Everything costs too much. Haiti doesn't have free schools. There isn't any soup kitchen you go to for food. There aren't any government food stamps either. Food, gas, education—it's all very hard to come by.

About six months ago, things were really hard. My small business renting out bikes didn't bring in much money. I just didn't have enough funds to get the business going. Then my mom died in Florida. We hadn't been in touch for a while. I only heard about it because a friend saw a post on Facebook and hit me up. He said, "I'm sorry your mom died." I wasn't surprised. I knew from the way she was living that she'd pass away. She had old-people sicknesses, diabetes and high blood pressure and such. I'm not exactly sure what she died of, but I think it might have been coronavirus.

I've got three brothers in Florida: William, Howard, and Wilgems. Howard's in jail. I heard he had been selling drugs out of my mom's house. Wilgems, he's the one with the restaurants, he thinks he's better than all of us. He wasn't helping out with my mom at all. But William had problems with depression. He died about six months before my mom died. I'm not sure what happened, maybe suicide.

Here's the thing. Even if we weren't in touch at the end, my mom made me tough. She told me, "You've seen me. I've never asked anyone for money. You're a grown man. No matter what problems you have, no matter where you are, I'm not ever going to give you more than $100." She never showed up to court, to my deportation hearing, nothing. My mother, she never smiled. You know, she never once told me she loves me. She was always saying mean things. Money is good, but it can't buy love. It can't buy happiness. She was never proud of me for anything I ever did. Yeah, she made me tough. Sometimes it would have been better for her to talk to me as a mother to son.

Wilgems, he's my mom and my dad's first son. He was with me on my voyages from Haiti to the

Bahamas and back to Haiti. The day after my mom died, he called and told me that my mom had left me $7,800. I knew she had a life insurance policy. She said that when she died, she'd leave me money. But I thought it was going to be more. Wilgems sent me the papers, but it was so complicated. That money was hard for me to get. After a few months, after a lot of struggle, with the help of my friend Joe Mozingo, who works for the *Los Angeles Times*, they finally gave me the money.

So things were starting to lighten up with the help of the money from my mother. I was able to do some things I'd been waiting on, like fixing up my house. I was preparing to send my kids to better schools. My wife needed a surgery. Now we had the money to pay for that. Things were looking up for us.

Word got around the neighborhood. They see you're not working but you're eating. They see a truck drop off fresh water at your house. They see you rent a car for a couple of days. They see you bring home a pizza. They see you start gaining weight. In Port-au-Prince, you can't get fat, because then people start to think you have money. And you don't talk to anybody about money, either.

Somebody must have gone and told the gangsters, *There's a guy around here with some money*. It could have been anybody.

One day my eight-year-old son, Diego, was out riding around on his bike with his friend, the two of them together on the bike. Some guys came and knocked the boys off the bike. They took Diego. Gangsters, they kidnapped my son. I was just down the block. I saw it happen, but I didn't get a good look at them. They had on those Scarface bandannas that hid their faces. About six or seven guys.

A couple of days later they called me and asked for $150,000 US. I said I didn't have that kind of money.

They hung up. About a week later one of the kidnappers called me up and asked me how much I had. I told them, and we made a deal. I went to the bank and took out most of the money I had left, $7,000. They held Diego for seventeen days. And if I hadn't been smart, they would have killed him.

The day we arranged for me to hand over the ransom money, I met one of the kidnappers in an area called Tokyo, near Cité Soleil. This guy recognized me from when I used to take journalists into Cité Soleil. I'm pretty well known for my work with international journalists. Some people think I can make them famous or something. This guy says, "Listen, they're going to take your money but they aren't going to give back your son." "Why?" I said. "Because they want more money." Then he says, "Listen, it's not fair. I'm going to help you out." So I gave him the money and together we went into Cité Soleil, into a real shady-ass neighborhood. Total slum. And he points to the house where they're holding Diego and says, "I'm going to go talk to the big boss. Go get your kid." Then he told me another route to get out of that neighborhood.

And so that's what I did. I started walking toward the house. I could hear these guys arguing. The guy who took my money said, "It's not fair, man. The guy paid." The house was raggedy. A country house, like made of mud and cow leather. The door was falling off. Normally, there would have been guards in front of it, but the guards were over by the big boss and they were all arguing about the money. So I took my chances and went inside. Lots of people, prisoners, were stuffed in there. I found Diego lying on the floor like he was dying. When he saw me he was happy, his eyes lit up, but he couldn't talk. You ever seen someone in shock? He couldn't walk, either. I picked him up and carried him out of there. He was so light from not eating. I carried him home. To this day, he doesn't remember what happened. But often at night he wakes up screaming and yelling. What can I do? I stay up with him until he calms down.

I finally had some money, and then somebody kidnapped my son. Then the same people that did the kidnapping, they took my house. These guys took lots of houses on my side of the street. The ones they didn't take, they burned. They are still living in my house today. All my money was taken away. I don't have a home. I don't have enough money to start a proper business. Would you want to stay in this place?

First, I had to get Diego out of there, or they'd probably take him again. I didn't have any money to get him a passport. So I sent him ahead to family in Cap Haitien, and from there, our family hired a passer to take him into the Dominican Republic. You give the passer like $200 US, and he pays the bus driver to give a little money at each immigration stop. There's seven stops. When immigration comes on the bus, they act like they don't see you. Sometimes they take people across the border through the bushes. That's how Diego came, through the bushes. All I know is that he arrived in the DR okay. So Diego is now with my oldest daughter, Esperanta, in the Dominican Republic. Esperanta is my wife's daughter. The first time I met her, she was eighteen months old. So really she's my daughter too. My daughter Medjine is also in the DR. Not legally, though.

I'm kind of worried right now because I'm not working. And the only funds that I'm able to get now come from begging my friends Joe and Peter. I know one day that's all going to stop.

Nothing's easy. You can't get a passport without money. You can't eat without money. In order to get help from people, I'm always having to ask. Whoever will help, I'll ask. Sometimes I even get help from my wife's sister who's living all the way in Brazil. My final plan, someday, is to try and move us all to Brazil. But that's going to take a lot of money. Where am I going to get it?

Good morning. This is me, Jean Marseille, doing a small recording about the terrible things that happened last night. You see, there's this group led by a guy called Vitelhomme. It's his own personal gang. They operate directly behind the American embassy. I'm sure they can hear all the fighting from the embassy. The street and an open field are all that separate the embassy from Vitelhomme. It's that close. But that embassy is so secure. Nobody can go in there. And once you get in there, you'd have no problem getting food. They have underground tunnels, all kinds of weapons. They could take out Vitelhomme in twenty-four hours, but they don't.

Vitelhomme's gang is in a conflict with another gang, called the 400 Mawozo, which are based around Croix-des-Bouquets. That's the place where Wyclef Jean comes from. The other night, Vitelhomme sent his gang members to make a kidnapping for ransom money. Well, as they were crossing the American embassy area, guess what? Vitelhomme's guys, they got kidnapped instead, and by the 400 Mawozo.

You understand what I'm saying? Gang kidnapped gang.

It's incredible that this type of stuff is going on so close to the American embassy! And that's around the same area where MINUSTAH* was based in 2004. There used to be a lot of security in this area. Not anymore.

I used to work in the slums with Joe Mozingo. He used to write stories about what was happening here with the gangs. That was during the time of Aristide.

---

* The United Nations Stabilization Mission in Haiti

I've still got a lot of contacts with gang members across the city. When they see me, they tell me what's happening. Some of these guys, they know they're not going to live for long. They want to go down in history. They want people to hear their story.

This is what I heard on the street. One of Vitelhomme's guys that was kidnapped had $400,000 US on him. The 400 Mawozo took the money and killed him, along with two or three of his friends. That's when Vitelhomme sent a message begging them, *You know what? Just give me back the bodies of the guys that you killed and we'll call it quits.* He didn't even want the money.

But the 400 Mawozo didn't give the bodies back. In Haiti, when you kill a body, you can't give it back, because of that mystical stuff. So they burned up those bodies. I know it's not safe to say this, but this guy, Vitelhomme, he's getting more and more powerful. He's mystical. He won't die. You can shoot him but his body won't take in the bullets.

So these two gangs, they're in a war. Vitelhomme, he's really strong now. And it seems like now the 400 Mawozo are losing, because last night around twelve houses were burned down in their area. A lot of gang members and also a lot of innocent people were killed. It's hard to get pictures of these things. It's not safe to get close. I hope you are starting to understand the types of things that are going on. The victims, they're the ones that come and tell me about this stuff. Do you see why I need to get my family out of here?

The other day, my wife and three of my kids tried to cross the border to the DR. My wife has proper papers and a visa and things like that. They accepted her and my daughter Annesamma and my adopted daughter, Geyonce, because they are underage. But they wouldn't let in my son MacDonald, because he is already eighteen. They said he needs his own passport. So the whole family turned back. My wife and daughters went to Cap Haitien. It's safer and we have family there. My wife sent MacDonald back to me in Port-au-Prince to try and get a passport. We're scattered all over now.

I'm trying to get MacDonald's papers done. The plan is for the whole family to meet in the DR soon, but who knows if it will all work out?

I have the strong belief that I'm still here struggling for a reason. I just don't know what the reason is. Lately I feel like I'm living strictly on faith. I lost my house and I don't have anything. I can't provide for my family. I'm here with one son, MacDonald. My wife, Anne-samma, and Geyonce are in Cap Haitien. My oldest kids are in the DR. David is in the DR, doing his own thing. I don't know exactly where he is. Esperanta and Medjine are taking care of my son Diego. He has some health problems after what happened to him. And I'm thinking, What's the next step after I get to the DR? I don't plan on staying in the DR for a long time.

But I have to go to the DR. Here there's no way to make money except to work on a farm. That's not my kind of work. I do city kind of work. Translation, driving, working for journalists. I like to do my own businesses, sell whatever's popular: clothes, tennis shoes, food items. This city's not safe to do any of this. The only choice is for us all to relocate to the Dominican Republic. But I want my house back, you know?

* * *

It's very hard for me to go to sleep. You understand where I'm sleeping? Right now, I'm staying in Delmas 19, in one of these small houses with an old tile roof. It's been raining, and the roof leaks. It gets wet where we sleep on the floor. I have a blanket I put on the ground, and one to sleep under, and when it rains, I have to wait until the floor dries before I can put my blanket down. That's when we can find a place to lie down. It's crowded in this place. MacDonald's doing better than I am. He blends in. He's a worry-free type of guy. Whatever situation he's in, he always laughs it out.

The guys that let us sleep here stay up all night. They smoke weed, smoke crack. Some of the people that stay here are in the gangs. I'm not going to judge. I only need a place to be for myself and my son.

I've seen a lot of people die. I lived through the earthquake of January 12. But these days, since the president was assassinated, the killings haven't stopped. Now people will kill you just for a misunderstanding about something you said. Or you might get killed for liking someone that's in power. Or you get killed just for trying to survive. Yesterday, in this neighborhood, this guy, he walked into a young girl's house and told her father, "Make sure you bring this girl to my house tonight so I can do whatever I want with her." The girl escaped. But guess what? I'm sorry to say that the guy killed the girl's father. The young girl, his daughter, she's still on the run.

It's raining right now. I'm standing in this rain to make this recording. I have a nice house. Those crooks took it for themselves. Now I've got to suffer it out in the rain.

The reason that Port-au-Prince is the way it is, the overwhelming suffering that's going on right now, is that even the people who have guns in their hands don't have enough to eat. They have to find a way to eat with that gun. Because there ain't no working here. There ain't no choice out here, either. You can either slave yourself to death or you find yourself a gun.

I'm from the United States; I know guns. I've seen them. You've got to make a choice. I don't have the heart to rob and kill people. I'd be destroying their family. I can't do that. You know some things you just can't do? The guys that are doing all that, they are going to die in a really ugly way. Why would someone want to be hated after their death? I believe in the afterlife. I feel like you never really die. Your soul goes into another body or another animal. I just don't like hurting people, even after they do something wrong. I'm not the bloodshed type.

The bourgeoisie—the people with the money upstairs, in the big places up in the hills—they're not going to allow any poor person to get up. There's no middle class in Haiti. You're rich or you're poor. The gangs that you see around Port-au-Prince are controlled by the bourgeoisie with all the money. Somebody is paying these gangs off, getting them guns. The gangs get together with all kinds of people from the government—the deputies, the magistrates, the prime ministers, the president, when there is a president, and these people control the ports, where things come in on the boats. They allow all the guns and all the bullets to go through. Big containers full of what we call "pèpè"—used clothes from people in the United States—come into Haiti all the time. Weapons and guns can be wrapped up real nice inside these clothes and smuggled in. Understand?

But the big mistake the bourgeoisie made is they put too many heavy weapons in the hands of these guys in the slums, these guys in the ghetto. Now there's no way of stopping what's going on. Today it's totally out of hand. Gangs have taken over Haiti.

There's something like forty-eight gangs. I can only name the popular ones. In Martissant, you got Izo and 5 Segonn. Izo is a young guy, about twenty-seven years old. He's the leader behind the 5 Segonn gang. Izo's a rapper, known all over Facebook. Haitians that live abroad listen to his music. They think he's just a rapper. They don't know that everything he talks about in his music, all the killing and whatnot, he's done it. He's not just singing about it. You know? Then you have Krisla, a gang leader. This Krisla is a well-dressed type of young man. He's from Tibwa. Then you have these guys from Grand Ravine. I don't go there. I'm just telling you what I hear. Then you have the ones they call Ti Lapli. These are the three or four popular ones around Martissant. I have people in there, but I don't go in those areas. And there's many more gangs in Baillergeau and Cité Soleil and Delmas 6 and Ouest and Saint Martin. All these areas are controlled by gangs. Delmas 6 is where this guy Barbecue is located. He's got a large following now. Barbecue was a cop. He used to do dirty jobs for the dead president Jovenel Moïse. Then you have the other side of the area, which are the 400 Mawozo. I told you about them and their fights with Vitelhomme. And the news lately is that Vitelhomme's gang is now the most powerful in Port-au-Prince. He's been sending envelopes with bullets to make sure that everybody around knows who's the big boss. Everyone that has a business has to pay up to G30,000 or G40,000 monthly for protection from him and other gangs. But every day, there are more gangs. They've been growing all over the country. Everybody has their thing they have to do to survive. In the cities, in the rural areas. Some gangs operate near the border.

There's gang soldiers around there that rob any vehicle coming through at one, two in the morning. People say that the 400 Mawozo, led by Lamo Sanjou, kidnapped sixteen Americans and one Canadian. You heard about it. CNN, BBC, everybody had it. But it wasn't the 400 Mawozo, it was Vitelhomme who took the Americans and the Canadian.* He's the one with the education, with the strategy. Vitelhomme made the plan, and he made a deal with Lamo Sanjou. Later, Vitelhomme and the 400 Mawozo would have conflicts. The reason for that kidnapping was to try to get Yonyon, the founder of the 400 Mawozo, out of prison by making an exchange for hostages. Yonyon was in prison for some things he did back in the day. But Lamo Sanjou and Vitelhomme got greedy and decided to make a different exchange. They were saying to themselves, "Yonyon is not going to be out of jail anytime soon, so we're just gonna take over. We're going to be the ones leading everything here." So instead they asked for $1 million for the sixteen Americans and the one Canadian. Well,

---

* Seventeen Canadian and American missionaries were abducted in October 2022.

Yonyon, in prison, when he heard about that deal, he got upset, because he said, "I just want to be out, and you release them for money?" The whole time, everybody was thinking the United States would intervene to save the hostages. But it never did. After the Haitian government gave the money, the kidnapped people all went home to America and Canada. Now the United States has put a warrant out for Vitelhomme and Lamo Sanjou. But here's the thing I can't understand: Why does America have to put warrants out when America has the power to just go in and get them? Why do the FBI, the CIA, and the American government leave these guys around to do crimes, kidnap, rape, and kill—and take people's homes?

I don't know why. I've been trying to understand since I was a little kid and went to America: Why does America not let Haiti evolve? Is it because of the color of our skin? The US leaves the Dominican Republic alone. It gets involved in our government. It gets involved in our elections. I think America is still pissed off that Haiti did that revolution back in the 1800s. And we're neighbors. We're that close. Why the hell do we have to speak French when we live a boat ride away from America?

Instead, America sends us guns. America makes its money out of war. Guns and bombs. All these guns are coming from America.

DISPATCH: 11/7/22

Maybe stories about this place are too much. You don't know where to start. Like today. A flood of people came running toward the Delmas 73 section—that's the section where I'm staying now. They were running because of the massive killing that's been going on in Canaan and those areas. Regular people, living in their homes with their kids. A woman came to my house— she was running with her kid and a few personal belongings. Her sister is a good friend of my wife's. Some gang members were burning houses, chopping

61

people up with machetes. And the people, they were just running.

Let me try to explain Canaan. In 2011, Sean Penn, the Red Cross, Oxfam, and many other organizations from all over the world got together to try and help all the people who were still homeless from the earthquake of January 12, 2010. A year after, tens of thousands of people were still living in camps in the city center and Delmas. This was when President [René] Préval was still in power. So the Haitian government and all these international organizations put their heads together and decided to build big camps for these people in the north part of the city, near the sea. These camps were supposed to be temporary, five years maximum. But it's 2022, and guess what? They're still there.

The Haitian people gave their own names to these places: Onaville. Jerusalem. Canaan. Names from the Bible. They called the area the Promised Land. Some people even built houses. Back in the day, it was a very beautiful place because it's by the sea, near where the boats come in. But now Canaan is no promised land. It's the dead land. It's the people-dying land. What's been happening is there's a deputy minister—some deputy minister of something, and he's responsible for Canaan and the surrounding areas—and he decided it's time to get rid of everybody. I guess he wants the land. There are beaches up there. Maybe he thinks one day it could be like a tourist attraction or something.

And in Canaan you've got this gang leader operating, Izo. I told you about Izo and his gang, 5 Segonn. What I hear is that Izo is working with the deputy minister, trying to get rid of people. Izo's doing the deputy minister's dirty work. That's how it works. Suddenly there's lots of killings. Izo sends his group led by one of his guys, Jeff, some guy they gave power to, into Canaan and other camps, and they start slaughtering people. And these poor people, they have nowhere to go. They just start running. They lost their houses in the earthquake. The government made them all sorts of promises. They tried to make a life up there. And now they're running again.

That's what's going on in Canaan, the Promised Land.

Ever since our president was murdered, things have been crazy. The government can't control the gangs. And the gangs are doing their best to get all they can before it's all over.

Now a lot of people in Haiti are talking about a military intervention. It's the elites and this new prime minister, Ariel Henry, who have been calling for the US and Canada to come in with soldiers. But the population doesn't trust Ariel Henry to make these decisions, because he wasn't elected. Some say Ariel Henry was put in power by the American government. The people didn't vote him in, and nobody understands how he came to power. So maybe he's a puppet of the United States. As long as he's in power, he's going to do exactly what the US wants him to do, not what the Haitian population wants him to do. Some feel like he had a part in the killing of President Moïse.

In Haiti, the elites and the government are one. People who work in the government don't always have money, but they run these big campaigns to get elected. Somebody's paying for those, right? So the government is controlled by the people with the money, the elites, the bourgeoisie—they are the ones with all the big money. The Haitian people think that if the elites want an intervention, it must be to help them get even richer. It's always good for the elites when people come from America and Canada. They stay in the nice hotels and spend money where the elites own things. I think that's the problem that Canada and America are having right now, because they don't know what to do. Would they be coming in to help the population? Or would they be coming in to help the elites, the ones who control everything already?

Haiti needs to get another country to give us support. It needs someone to come in and help rebuild. America, with its good architects, the professional engineers, the good builders, to work to help rebuild the buildings and houses. Haitians are good workers, and after a while, they will be building their own houses. And they've got to get the population to replant trees. Trees are going to calm down the heat and give out more oxygen. And we don't have trees, because they cut down trees to make charcoal. Our biggest problem is that we import everything and don't export.

But the US has no plans to help Haiti. The US needs war because it makes money selling guns. The US doesn't care if it's the good guys or the bad guys. It sells guns.

Listen, Peter, I sent you a video of a young guy being tortured, burned with melted plastic. Did you get it? His name is Fritz-Jean Wilson. He's twenty-one years old and he was... It's terrible. Real nice guy. Fritz was kind. He grew up with us. He was younger, but he was around all the time. He had dreams of going to the States. He wanted to be a big-time basketball player. And he's not a guy that's into any gang violence. He didn't really care about anything but having a good time. It could be one o'clock in the morning and we could say, *Fritz, we need some cigarettes, man*, and he'd go get them. And he could cook anything with a small amount of money. Sometimes, if he didn't have anywhere to stay, I'd put him up for a few days. He liked me because I speak English and he was trying to learn.

I didn't know what happened to Fritz until the other night when I was talking to a friend of mine. I was explaining that I was trying to get out of here, planning to go to the DR. And he told me, "Man, whatever you do, don't go illegally. Look what they did to Fritz."

About nine or ten days ago, Vitelhomme and his group were having problems again with the 400 Mawozo. Soldiers in the 400 Mawozo near the border were robbing people. They didn't know, but they took money from Vitelhomme's people. So Vitelhomme's guys got together and wiped out a whole area by the airport. They burned down every house and massacred as many people as they could. Fritz lived in that neighborhood. Lucky for him, when the burning occurred, he wasn't home. Everybody at his house was killed. His mother, his father. All his relatives.

Even before the war between Vitelhomme and the 400 Mawozo, Fritz had a lot of people that were after him. He was a freeloader. He talked too much about things he wasn't supposed to talk about. And I heard something crazy: he went to the witch doctor, and whatever the witch doctor did, Fritz thought he couldn't get shot by bullets. My friend told me that Fritz escaped the burning houses and reached the area around Malpasse on the north side of town. He probably paid somebody to take him there. Unfortunately, he must've gotten caught in the bushes trying to cross into the Dominican Republic. My friend didn't know exactly what happened. All we know is that these guys took Fritz's phone and they videoed the torturing they did to him. They sent the video to all his friends on his Facebook.

We never got any more messages after that one with the video. This is what happens to the young people in Haiti when they get caught up in this stuff and they run away. They get caught up between Haiti and the DR. This thing is very disturbing. I've lost so many people. Someway, somehow, I've always managed to stay alive in Port-au-Prince. But now I just want out of here. It hurts me to death to have to be here. I haven't slept all night, again. There's no safety anywhere here. As I speak to you now, I don't know where Fritz is.

I don't know if he's dead or alive.

Good afternoon. [*Coughing*] I'm sorry. This is going to be a short recording.

I don't really want to leave. But things keep getting worse and worse. I don't know if I'm going to live to see the day I get out of here, because things are taking so long. If I am going to stay here, I just want to live somewhere that is decent, so I don't have to be on the streets.

Look, I'm sleeping on the streets. That's how I ended up on the plaza, the one by the airport, the park that

President Martelly made, where I'd lay my head to sleep. A lot of people were sleeping there.

[*Coughing*] I'm super sick. My mom passed away in the States. My brother Wilgems don't give a fuck. Excuse my language. And I'm not sleeping well. I have a blanket. This woman saw me sitting on the plaza and I guess felt kind of bad for me—she gave me a blanket. [*Coughing*]

I didn't want to do this recording. I didn't want you to hear how sick I am. But I guess I have no choice. Because it's very important that you guys hear me. I'm getting old. I'm fifty-some years old now. I can't be going on like this. I have to get myself stabilized. And I have these kids coming up. I gotta prepare for their future. But here in Haiti, I just feel like I'm wasting time.

Tonight is different. This woman let me stay in her backyard. She's an older woman, maybe in her fifties. She'd cook food by the side of the road. Regular Haitian plates with sauce and rice and beans and a little bit of chicken or pork. She served all the people from the factories. I came around three or four to buy food, but this time she saw I was still there around seven, and she knew it wasn't like me to still be around the plaza. She asked what was wrong, and I told her there was some trouble around my neighborhood. She took me and let me stay in her backyard, in a log cabin thing without a door. And I'm still cold as heck. I have this fever. She made me some tea. It made me feel better. If I ever get a chance for a better life, I would come back to Haiti to sell my house. I know gangs can't rule forever. I don't know how long all this is going to last. I love Haiti. But the point where it's gotten right now, it's like a lot of love lost. You know what I mean? Like love wasted.

This recording's gotten to a point. It's me, Jean Marseille. Today is November 20, 2022. Thank you very much. Have a good night.

Good morning, Laura. Good morning, Peter. Good morning, any other person that might be listening to this recording. Today is a big, special day for me. Even though I'm not completely well, I made it to this point. The fever has been down. I'm feeling better. And I'm packing my things as we speak right now to get ready to go meet my family in Cap Haitien.

This recording could be much longer, but my phone doesn't have a lot of charge, because the hotel that I slept in last night doesn't have electricity. It's not like a hotel you see in the US. A small room, one or two beds, you go outside to use the restroom, there's no running water.

I've been up all night. And I'm really nervous just waiting to meet my kids and my wife.

I went to the doctor, got my medication. It's about four thirty now, I'm about to head out. MacDonald has his papers done. I got my passport made. Now we're going to catch a ride to get to Cap Haitien to go meet my family.

Only thing I can say is that this was the roughest experience I have had in my lifetime. Living on the streets. For the last couple of weeks, I've been really sick, but I'm getting better now because of happiness. Knowing that the whole family will be together forced my body to get better. I just know that when I see all my kids together, I'm gonna feel even better.

I've been on the phone with my wife all day, all night. She's been helping me prepare over the phone. I bought myself a suitcase. I wasn't able to buy things, like clothes and stuff like that, because I wanted to reserve some money so when I get to Cap Haitien, I can take my family out to eat and spend that last day with them before I go to the Dominican Republic.

The thing that really hurts me is that I have to leave my two daughters and my wife, not knowing when I'm going to get the money to get them across the border to join me.

My experience in Port-au-Prince was devastating. It was like a horror movie. I don't know how I survived. You think at any time someone is going to hurt you. All through the night. It's not like you have a better place to go, and somebody is going to give you a place to stay. You can't trust anybody. People come up to you late at night and wake you up just to ask you for water. Water. I thought I was doing okay, and then everything was just falling loose. You think you're doing okay, and then somebody can come along and just take everything.

I'm thanking all the people that stayed by my side to make sure this could become a reality, to get out of this situation I'm in, the position I live in every day, risking my life, trying to stay alive.

I should be in Santiago in two days.

SANTIAGO DE LOS CABALLEROS

DISPATCH: 12/1/22

On December 1, 2022, Jean sent us a recording before he legally crossed the border into the Dominican Republic.

I'm on the bus now, like an hour away from the border. I'm almost out of Haiti. The bus is almost totally empty. I think there are about six of us. Everyone has visas and passports, and that's the only way you can possibly go into the DR legally. Illegally would be a different way.

I'm happy that I finally got myself to this transportation for getting out of Haiti to a better place. But

I'm asking myself, Is it really a better place? I don't have plans to stay in the DR. I really wanted to go to Brazil or Costa Rica.

My wife and my two daughters are left back in Cap Haitien, sadly. My wife didn't feel too good about me leaving without her, but I guess I had no choice. I'm planning to get myself settled and find a way to get my daughters passports and visas and get them and my wife to the DR, so I can have all the family in one place. I'm unhappy that I had to leave them behind, but I have the others in my family waiting for me to arrive in Santiago.

Jean traveled to Santiago de los Caballeros, the second-largest city in the Dominican Republic. He is staying on the city's outskirts with his oldest daughter, Esperanta. Jean's other family members in the Dominican Republic include his daughter Medjine, who works in a cigar factory with Esperanta and is engaged to a Dominican man; and David, Jean's oldest son, whom he doesn't hear from much. David paints advertisements for a living and is a little bit wild, as Jean describes him. Also in Santiago is Jean's youngest son, Diego, whom Jean sent away to the DR from Port-au-Prince to live with Esperanta, after

Diego was kidnapped and held for ransom. Diego, in the aftermath of his kidnapping, is suffering from an injury that is assumed to be from someone hitting him over the head with a gun or other blunt object. Because Diego cannot recall the events of the kidnapping, no one can be sure of the origin of the head wound.

Doctors said that Diego's injuries were causing swelling and putting pressure on his brain, but they needed to do blood work and imaging to be sure where to operate. Luckily, much medical care is available for free in the DR. However, some necessary aspects of care, such as diagnostic testing, must be conducted at private clinics that charge for services. In March of 2023, after an agonizing period of watching Diego suffer, Jean was able to come up with the money to get Diego the surgery he needed. Soon after, Jean sent an update.

I borrowed some money from my job to pay for Diego's blood work and scan, $230 US. So they keep $60 every week for four weeks to pay off the loan. They have me pay interest. It's fair to make me pay interest, but it's bad for me because I had to do what I had to do to get my son out of the hospital. So from now until the loan is finished, every time I get paid, I only get $20.

Diego's happy that I'm around. We're very attached. He's pacing around this house with me as I talk. He's better now. He's not doing great yet, but he's doing better. He still has headaches. He's remembering. And he's back in Dominican school.

| *We hear from Jean again on March 24, 2023, his birthday.*

Hello, good morning. It's early in the morning. Today's my birthday. I have a place to sleep right now because my oldest daughter got herself together to help her old man. And I'm very happy it's my birthday. I thank the Lord for making me live to see fifty-two years old. Wow. And I feel healthy, and I feel good, and I have a place to stay. I get to take a shower and wash my clothes. I'm not comfortable, but I'm okay, I'm okay. And hopefully I get something to eat today.

| *Later:*

My daughter Esperanta bought some wine and some Presidentes and some plantains and we just danced it out. Took a bunch of photos.

Soon after, Esperanta helps Jean find work using his English skills in a call center contacting US citizens about Medicaid add-on programs. Jean rents a house for himself and three of his children to share. He works around ten hours per day. Some days he can't afford transportation to work, adding an additional three to four hours of walking to his day.

The job pays my rent and puts food on the table, but not every day. I get paid about $80 per week. I've got to have $80 for food for a week. You buy salami, you buy chicken, you buy bread, toilet paper. You have to pay the light bill. A cab ride to work costs different prices. If you take an Uber, it's going to cost $4 US. You take a moto, it'd be about $1.50. If you go in a concho, the taxi is $0.35.* But when you get off work at eight o'clock at night, you definitely have to have a hundred pesos in your pocket to get home. If I do have some money, I need to buy some food. Half the time, I have to walk to work, thinking I'll get exercise.

---

* Concho cabs, or taxis, run on regular routes and pick up several passengers at a time.

So I don't really have any time to be on the streets, you know, to be getting in trouble or hassles with anyone. I don't go out, I don't go to movies, I don't do anything. The only life I have in the DR is going to work. Then I come back home and speak to my family over the phone. In the neighborhood where I live, the Dominican people always make some kind of remark to show you that they don't want you around. If you wave, they're not going to wave back. So I don't hang around on the streets. I keep to myself.

In April, months into his time in the DR, working overtime, Jean is still not able to afford all his family's necessities: paying for rent and food for himself and two of his seven children, Medjine and Diego, and sending some money to his wife, Guerda, who still lives in Haiti with three of their children. Not to mention education, visas, and transportation costs.

MacDonald, Annesamma, Geyonce, and my wife are still with my wife's sister in Cap Haitien. They are living in one small room. Annesamma says she has to sleep on the ground. Everybody just squeezes themselves in. They're just trying to survive until they get here. Because the best solution is to have my entire family here with me, my wife and all my kids. Only then will I feel safe. I'm waiting on the money so I can send for them. Everything is on pause right now until I get the money.

Jean has work, housing, and a relatively stable environment. Still, troubles accumulate. His wife and daughters are not safe in Haiti. Historical tensions between Haiti and the Dominican Republic compound with fresh, contemporary wounds.

When I wake up in the morning here, I am so cold, and I am so sad and depressed. I just want to go home. But I don't want to leave here with nothing in my hands and go home and starve. I've got to be honest: things are not good here. The Dominicans have all the power over Haitians. They mistreat us because they know they can. They know our country is at war right now and we're fighting among ourselves. They know we have no choice but to suffer. They're very racist toward Haitians. The situation with Haitians and Dominicans goes way back. I only know what I hear from people around, from what my kids learn in school. I learned American history in school because I went to school in Florida. [Jean-Pierre] Boyer, one of our first Haitian presidents, in the 1800s, mistreated the Dominicans. He forced them not to speak Spanish. These things stay with people. It doesn't matter how long ago it was. And Dominicans know they've got debts to us too. Like at the Massacre River, the Dominican government some years ago killed, like, thirty thousand Haitians and threw them into that river. That's why they call it "the river of massacre."*

The thing I miss the most about Haiti is that my family, my wife and my kids, were around me and always expressing so much love to me. Before my house was taken, I was okay, because I had a little business that I used to do. I was living in my house with many rooms and my family. When I woke up in the morning in Haiti, it was like the sunshine to me, you know, and I'm free.

---

* "The Massacre River in northeastern Haiti was the site of a 1937 massacre of thousands of Haitians by Dominican dictator Rafael Trujillo. It takes its name, however, from a bloody battle between French and Spanish colonists in the 1700s."
　　　　　　　　　　　　　　—Jacqueline Charles, *Miami Herald*

On July 11, 2023, Jean messages with alarming news.

My young daughter Annesamma, she was sexually harassed by my wife's sister's husband, so she ran away and called me from some woman's phone asking for help. I am trying to get her to the DR.

> *Jean, to this day, does not want to talk about what happened to Annesamma in her aunt's home and after she ran away from it. The day after she fled, Annesamma was attacked by gang members and hospitalized. Jean suggested that the attack had been a sexual assault.*

I'm with my daughter Medjine, who speaks Spanish very well. We are in the Dominican Republic now, at the border between Haiti and Santiago, a place called Dajabón. Tomorrow morning, Medjine and I are going to check in our passports at the border. We'll go to the Haitian side and then check back into the Dominican side. I haven't checked in for two months, so I have to pay extra fees for missing that month. The regular fee is $20, but when you're late, they make you pay $50 more. So that's about $70 US I have to pay.

And I just pray that we make it home tomorrow with Annesamma. Sometimes the voyage is risky, especially for girls. We're going to leave Annesamma at a hotel and the passers are going to come and pick her up, and we're all going to leave on the same bus, okay? And there's going to be, like, eleven stops at immigration. Immigration comes on the bus—they check the Haitians, and if you're not correct, they deport you back to Haiti. So every stop we go to, we have to give a bribe to the Dominican immigration police that check the buses. Then they pretend they don't see Annesamma.

Annesamma didn't make it to the DR on that attempt.

DISPATCH: 7/24/23

I think I'm going on eight months out here. The first three months were the hardest for me. I was afraid to be out on the streets. I was always getting humiliated. One time, I tried to take a concho, a taxi, and the driver told me he wouldn't take Haitians. I don't speak Spanish, so I am confused a lot of the time. Maybe someone tries to tell you in a packed cab that the door isn't closed right, but you don't understand, and everybody yells at you. Or you don't know the city and you get suckered. I don't know how the average Haitian who doesn't speak English gets by out here. My English helps me.

There's much more to my story, but there are some things I can't reveal, because it's just so painful. Some things I can't explain to you. Nobody wants to reveal 100 percent of what's happened to them. Like what happened to Annesamma in Haiti—please, I can't tell it to you. People don't get to hear about that. Annesamma is so happy to see me now. She told me about the difficult situation she just went through to get to the DR. My money wasn't right for me to get a visa for her. It would take up the little money I have. A visa for the DR for Haitian kids costs $650 US. So I had to pay a passer $300 US to try to get Annesamma from Cap Haitien to Santiago. They took her through the bushes, the route to cross the border. She said they had to turn around and go back to Haiti because of the immigration police. They wear civilian clothes, but they have a hat that says IMMIGRATION. You see what a young girl, my young daughter, has to go through?

Every morning that I wake up in the DR, I feel like a lost soul. I get very nervous and afraid, very sad and lonely. I feel like anything bad could happen to me. I'm insecure, I'm unsafe. The thing that worries me the most being in the DR is still having family back in Haiti, knowing that my wife's situation is not stable. It has changed for the worse since I've been there. The neighborhood where I used to live before they took my house has totally been taken over by Vitelhomme. The violence has moved to the north, to the east, to the south, and to the southeast. It's taken over the whole country. Everybody is trying to run out of Haiti. Dominicans are taking money from the Haitians to get them into the DR. But then once we are here, they mistreat us. And a lot of Haitians who've run to the DR are then getting deported. So they make money off us when we struggle to get here, and then they kick us out when they feel like it.

I've witnessed immigration cops ripping up a Haitian's passport. This was about two weeks ago when I was getting off work. I was with another Haitian who works the same job as me. He had an updated visa, everything was good. But the Dominican cops took his passport and shredded it. I was like, Wow. Do you know how difficult it is to get a passport in Haiti? I paid many times the people who made mine. I stayed in the immigration line for five or six hours. Then, when I couldn't take it anymore, I paid extra money to go to the front of the line. Because of President Biden's program that they have in the United States, there's too many people wanting passports.* Now you can't get a passport made. Even if you had $600 or $700 US, you still wouldn't be able to get a passport made.

And, look, some things are good. The Dominican Republic is a much cleaner place. Trucks pick up trash in the morning. It's a beautiful place. It's got big malls, you can go to the theater, there are yellow lines on the streets. It's got electricity in the houses. It has a working internet system. The weather is different between Haiti and the DR. It's very, very hot in Haiti because there aren't trees. Electricity is another thing about the Dominican Republic that I like. There's always less electricity in Haiti.

---

* On January 9, 2023, Biden's administration renewed an existing humanitarian parole program. Parole is granted if an urgent humanitarian need is found in a person's case. If granted humanitarian parole, a person may work in the US, but the program does not provide any permanent path to staying in the country.

But I was always a little bit happier in Haiti, when I was working and could get a little money to take care of my special needs and my family. I had my house with my family. It means a lot to me to have my own space. Another difference between Santiago and Port-au-Prince is I had a lot of respect in my neighborhood because I was a helpful person in the community. I had a lot of people that looked up to me.

A lot of Dominicans are poor too. They are on the streets begging, doing little businesses like they do in Haiti. They have mercados, these small markets where they sell food items just like they do in Haiti. They sell what you need, like beans, rice, plantains, toilet paper, cigarettes. And the jobs that are here, just like in Haiti—they don't pay much. The Dominican government is doing basically the same things to Haitian people that go on in Haiti. The Dominican government gives Dominican people the power to rule over us.

I know it's supposed to be better, but sometimes I feel fear like I did in Haiti. Can you imagine being around a lot of people that hate you because of your color? If I didn't open my mouth to speak English so they think I'm American, I don't think I'd find transportation to get to work, because they don't want their skin to touch Haitians.

This is not a place for a Black person. Any Dominican can do anything they want to a Haitian and get away with it. I see a lot of people getting bullied because they're Black. One day when I was going to work, I saw the immigration police take a woman's things. She was carrying them in a basket on top of her head. When you see somebody carrying things on their head like that, you automatically know that person's a Haitian. The police jumped off their moto and knocked over the basket on her head. Things fell out of the basket: tomatoes, beans. And then they took her away, didn't even ask for her papers.

At the same time, we share an island. Two nations condemned to live together. We do business together. The immigration guards—they're doing their job and they'll also take a little money. Deport somebody today, he'll come back tomorrow. Maybe an hour later. And he goes to the same guard. It's making money. They need Haitians to function. The sugarcane grown in the DR for the United States—mostly Haitians do that work. Because Haitians are real hard workers.

I heard on the news that the French were sending some military forces to try to help Haiti with the insecurity. But it never happened.

I wake up every morning and want to go back home. But what would I go back home to? I don't have a home. And my wife, she's not living safely in Cap Haitien. I would like to be with her, but if I go back to Haiti there's going to be more suffering because there's no work. There's no good choice, you know? I'd definitely rather make the choice to go back instead of being deported. Sometimes, when my wife is worrying about certain things she needs that she can't get, I just want to get up and run back over the border to her. It brings tears to my eyes. But I can't rush to Haiti, because I'm empty-handed.

Laura, I was thinking, do you think I could make a little cash if I put my story on YouTube? When I first got the job at JC Solutions, I made $80 per week. They gave me a promotion, but they're paying me only $3 an hour US. Now I work nine to six, five days a week, and get $150 per week.

I work at a place called JC Solutions. They're respectful to me because there are a lot of people from the States working there. The supervisor, Hugo, he's a deportee from the United States. He's from Brooklyn, New York.

He was selling drugs and got deported to the Dominican Republic. Even Carlos, the owner, was deported from the States. He started with making transfers, just like me. He got a contract from the United States for Medigap Life, the national center for Medicare benefits. It's the easiest program that they have to sell. It's the easiest script to say. And they don't have a problem with me there, because I always make the most transfers.

A transfer means that whenever you get someone interested in Medicare retirement benefits, you transfer them over to a licensed agent that's in their state to help them receive their benefits. You get incentives when you make over eighty-five transfers per week, and since the beginning, I've been making up to one hundred and twenty-five transfers per week. They found it remarkable, even the supervisor. Once he asked me, "What do you tell these people—that you're going to give them a Cadillac?" I don't know what it is about me that keeps people listening. Maybe because I have a Florida accent? Maybe it's because I've been around a bunch of journalists and writers and I feel confident. I know my English is good enough. I'm calling older people. I tell them good morning. I tell them I don't need their social security card or anything like that. I apologize for disturbing their day, and ask them how they're doing. And people tell me that I'm so polite they have to listen to me.

I can remember it without the script. This is how I do it:

> My name is Jean Pierre calling on behalf of Medigap Life. This call is about your Medicare benefits that will put more money toward your groceries and utilities in your home. Your food card, your flex card, your dental, vision, hearing, and over-the-counter benefits will be increased with no additional cost to you. Do you have Medicare part A and part B, the red, white, and blue card that gets you qualified to receive extra benefits with no additional cost to you?

Sometimes I try to figure out the person and switch the everyday speech around. Most of the time, they think it is a scam, or they're just not interested, or they already receive the extra benefits. People cuss me out all the time. Sometimes they don't even give you the chance to show you're a nice person. A lot of other insurance companies are calling them: United, Blue Cross Blue Shield, Anthem, Humana... all those places. They get aggravated, some people get emotional. So your English has to be up-to-date. You have to have a convincing voice to get people interested in buying the benefits, because there's so many scams on the computer and internet. I stay calm, and I'm polite to the agents when we transfer. Sometimes, after a transfer, I stay on the line to hear how the agents sell.

It's very difficult to get the number of transfers per day that they want you to make. If you make less than four transfers before noon, they automatically send you home. If you do the same thing on the third day, they automatically fire you. They post a list of how many transfers everyone makes. There's a lot of places that fire you for one mistake.

Yes. Hello. It's about 4:55 in the morning.

I have never been stable in my life, since I was born. Everyone that's living on earth wants to be from somewhere, wants to be part of something. As for me, since the age when I understood I was a human being, I haven't had a boundary. I don't have a nationality. I could say I'm proud to be Haitian, but I'm not really Haitian. Because I have an identity that I lost. I was Bahamian, but I don't have a birth certificate. I was born in the Bahamas. I've never been back to my homeland since I left when I was one, never experienced going to school where I was born. All my life, I've been a lost kid.

The United States is very important to me because I was raised there and I went to school there. I had a lot of friends. I have family who are American. I would love to go back to America, but because of being deported, there's a slim chance that I can get back to the States. I put that plan to the side and try not to worry about it, so I won't be so depressed.

I have never seen my actual birth certificate. That would be my best wish: to have my Bahamian birth certificate, to go back to the hospital in Freeport, Bahamas, where my mother and father said I was born, to discover what age I really am and exactly what day I was born. From what my mother told me, everyone that was born in the Bahamas has a birth certificate with a footprint on it. I was born in 1971, that is the probable year. I'm not sure exactly. My mom said around March time, so I just came up with a date. My dad said it was April, so I just picked March. And twenty-four, that's my favorite number. But I'm pretty sure I was born in 1971, and I know my parents' names: Jocelyn Pierre and Weldeck Marseille.

My life was not that great in Haiti, but it was not that bad either, for all those years. Now everything's unstable. I don't have a personal home and my visa will run out this December. I have to start thinking ahead. My health is going down. I want to prepare myself for the time when I get older and get sick. I have no savings. I worry about the days when I get older, because there's no social security and things like that in Haiti. These things worry me.

Yes, if I had a birth certificate saying that I'm Bahamian, I would be free somewhere they won't kick me out, because it's my place of birth. Then I could start a new life. Freeport, Bahamas—that's where I was born. That's my dream: to live in the Bahamas and move all my family there so we could live a better life. That would be my good start. But how do you get there?

I didn't get fired. To be exact, I did not get fired. I got sent home.

Last week, two of my coworkers were standing outside the business smoking cigarettes and speaking Kreyòl, and the immigration police put them in their truck and took them to jail. They were going to deport them, but Carlos, my boss, went and paid some money and they let them go. It's all a cycle. Making money, see what I mean?

This past Thursday, immigration came inside my work and they said there were too many Haitians working in the office. The law says when there's twenty Dominicans working, there can only be five Haitians working.

The next day the boss announced, "Okay, guys, whoever has a computer at your house, you're going to be working from home." Medigap Life will pay you a little extra to cover the internet. A basic internet connection is, like, $180 for the installation and $35 monthly, but then it can go out on you. And working from home, you can find a job that pays $7 an hour. I work and work, I know all these professional people, and I still can't afford a computer. I'm feeling like my plans have been destroyed, like I take one step forward and then two steps back.

You ask me what are my plans? Every week, the plan shifts. For example, my plan to go to the Bahamas and retrieve my birth certificate, that's going to take money.

I still want to find out how old I am and have a nationality and know I'm officially that person. But here I am. You ask me what my plans are?

Yesterday there was a big demonstration and a couple of Haitians were killed, shot in the streets. If it was Haiti, I would know more about it.

The Dominican Republic is now saying that it gives Haitians three months to leave the country. Many thousands of people are already being deported. Even if you have a passport or not, they don't want to hear it. There's no way to check in your passport, get a visa. And that's why a lot of Haitians are just taking their bags and leaving voluntarily. They go back to Haiti not knowing what the consequences are going to be. They're going back home because they're not wanted in the DR.

The canal that Haiti's making, there's going to be more work.* Like four hundred acres of land for farming? Not saying it's going to be better, but they're going to see if that land will work out so Haiti can feed itself. More people used to grow food in Haiti. The rainy season doesn't come around like it used to.

---

* In a dispute over water-access rights to the Massacre River on the two countries' northern border, the Dominican Republic closed its entire 220-mile border to Haiti. Haiti began work on a canal that will feed dry land with water for crop growth.

DISPATCH: 10/5/23

The border has been closed. So there's no way to go check in my passport. There's no way to renew my visa, the monthly fee I always pay. So passport or not, if you're Haitian, everyone's in hiding. I'm afraid to go outside. My kids are in the house with me. Everybody's panicking, we're afraid. There's inflation going on. Immigration has been deporting people twice as much as they were before. They drop people off in the middle of the streets in Haiti. I don't want to be deported in that animal condition.

I want to go to Haiti only because I have my wife there. And two kids. That's the only reason I want to go. I don't want to be forced to go. Even if you have a passport and you check in and everything—but the border is closed now, so you can't go check in. So it'd be best for me to leave on my own terms and have a chance to take some things back with me. I don't want to go back to Haiti with nothing.

Between Dominicans and Haitians, things are getting real frustrated and both sides are suffering. The Dominican president says he wants nothing to do with Haitians, business-wise, and immediately the Dominican Republic puts an embargo on Haiti. Haiti has decided it will not buy any products from the Dominican Republic. The Dominicans are losing thousands and thousands of dollars daily on the products they were selling to Haiti. The DR was the only place that Haiti was buying food from, like eggs, oil, bananas, plantains, rice, all the necessary food items that people need to survive. So right now in Haiti, one egg costs about $2 US, not to mention the price of oil and other things that were coming from the DR: food, car parts. People send their kids to college in the DR. There's

no college in Haiti that's functioning properly. Esperanta got two years of college in the DR. But I couldn't
continue to pay.

I am stuck because I don't have a computer. Otherwise I would spend the last three months of my stay
here working my job so I could earn some money to
take back to Haiti. It's the enrollment period for my
job—Americans age sixty-five or older can start their
benefits or increase them for the next year—so people
are even working on Sundays to earn extra money
before Christmas. And I think that's terrible because
I spent almost a year working there and I'm not able
to receive my Christmas bonus, which would've been
great for me to have in my hand on my way back to
Haiti. It hurts to see that I could work at the job, but
I can't even come up with $200 to buy a thing as simple
as a secondhand computer.

Diego, he's not a normal kid anymore. He has memory loss. Headaches. He stutters now. He still doesn't remember what happened in Port-au-Prince. He mumbles, and it takes him a long time to get the words out. He stutters and then he gets upset. He wakes up in the middle of the night and takes off running. I think he's having a flashback when that happens. Like he's in shock. Some people think he's a problem kid. I'm the only one who understands him. The teachers are saying he's not normal. He was in sixth grade but they had to move him back a year. He's in regular classes with other kids, but he's not the only one that has special needs. He has friends, but they beat him up. [*Coughing*]

Annesamma learned Spanish on TikTok and on Google, she goes on YouTube. She makes a lot of friends, nobody picks on her. She's beautiful, she looks Dominican, and she speaks the language. I got her into school, bought her books, got her clothes, paid the moto every day to take her back and forth to school. She is really smart at school. The school tested her and put her in a higher class for her age.

David went to Haiti to do some big-time billboard painting for some company that's opening in Haiti. I think it's an advertisement for paint.

MacDonald went back to Cap Haitien because he loves his mom and he wants to keep her safe. He works when he can. He does transport, takes people where they want to go on his moto, fixes bikes.

My dad is helping Esperanta get a sponsor to go over to the US on the Joe Biden plan. Esperanta's brother from her daddy is helping her apply for it too. She works in a fancy restaurant now. She's a cook, and she keeps burning herself at work.

In the house I have now, Diego is sleeping next to my bed in a small room. My son has to sleep on the floor. Annesamma is in the living room with Medjine. She doesn't have a way to be comfortable as a young lady. It isn't enough space for all of us. And the landlord is saying there are too many of us.

I'm just now making it home and nobody is cooking any food. With the financial difficulties, I'm having family issues. I can't keep the lights on, because my daughter will be complaining about the light bill. Even though Medjine is working, they only pay her, like, $40 a week. And I'm dodging my wife now because I only have enough money to pay rent. I can borrow 500 pesos on a paycheck from my work, and then you have to pay that back, plus 100 pesos. And every week you don't pay it back, the debt increases another 100 pesos.

It's personal to tell you that I need $100 to pay my rent. Because of the situation... I ask. I want to be self-reliant and independent because I'm a father.

It's too dark now. I can't keep the lights on, because of the mosquitoes. When I'm here in this small room with these mosquitoes, I think a lot. I'm not doing anything. I've been following the news, and from what I heard, the United Nations has a plan to send a group of soldiers from Kenya* to try to help out with the situation in Haiti, and maybe stop some of the

---

* Kenyan forces eventually arrived in late June 2024.

kidnapping and the crimes that occur every day. That makes me kind of happy and changes a lot of my plans. If the UN goes into Haiti, I won't have any choice but to go back home.

But I don't think it's a good idea to have a military force in Haiti. I hope it turns out better, but I doubt it. Outside military forces have come to Haiti before, like the US back in '94 and in 2000-something. They never solved anything. It just got worse. And more guns came into the country. So I think it's going to be the same thing happening again. What the Haitian population would like is for the old Haitian military to reestablish power and help stop the violence.

The police are so corrupt. So when Kenya comes, how are they going to distinguish who is corrupt from who is not? There has to be somebody who knows exactly who's who, because a lot of the Haitian police are working with the gangs.

I come out here and find tons of other problems. Now I'm afraid I'm going to be put out on the streets because every month I have to pay rent. I have no choice but to leave the DR or get caught in the streets and get deported. I can't get my family somewhere else.

Imagine: My wife has been complaining to me for months now that she can't buy food to eat. She doesn't have a stable place to live, she's moving around. She sent me pictures of her going to the hospital. She got really skinny. I don't talk to her often anymore, because there's not enough money to pay for her phone. When she is around someone who has a phone, she calls me on WhatsApp from different numbers at different times. Next month will be our anniversary, twenty-seven years of being married.

I'm not going to immediately just go back to Haiti. I'm going to wait a little bit to see if I can get my house back. I don't have any news about where I lived, because everybody left that neighborhood, and I lost communication with the people that lived there. If I hear people are coming back in my area, I will immediately leave to go pick up my wife in Cap Haitien or wherever she may be right now, and then try to figure out how to get some work. I'm just living as the day goes.

AFTERWORD

Beginning with our work on the oral history collection *Lavil: Life, Love, and Death in Port-au-Prince*, we (the editors) have been listening to Jean's story for over a decade. As Jean said of his telemarketing work, "I don't know what it is about me that keeps people listening." For me, I continue to listen because he doesn't provide easy answers, sometimes loses his patience, but in the end always, indefatigably, searches for meaning.

And his story continues. Soon after we last heard from Jean, he found work in another call center and was once again a top performer. But his debts had accumulated. In December of 2023, Jean sent another update.

I'm sorry to say that after the landlords took our money for the back rent, they still put us out. She took the money, and then she had her husband come tell me that we had to leave. I was sleeping on the streets last night. Now I'm the first one at work. And I understand why she put us out, because we were three months late to pay rent. I understand. Also she said there were too many of us living there. I just need to get a place to stay. I have to get my kids comfortable.

Jean's children Diego, Annesamma, and Medjine are staying in Santiago with a college friend of his oldest daughter, Esperanta. Jean's wife, their son MacDonald, and their adopted daughter, Geyonce, are still in Haiti. Jean has a few hundred dollars in his pocket—the deposit that he got back from his landlord—but he is saving the money for a down payment on a new place. So when we spoke one afternoon a few days after the eviction, he hadn't yet eaten that day. What kind of choice is that, between shelter and food? Not even shelter, just the hope to afford shelter in the near future. We talk so often I'm starting to sound like Jean.

As disputes grow between Haiti and the Dominican Republic, and scrutiny of Haitians in the DR increases, and Jean finds himself again without enough money to cover his expenses, he has begun to imagine another deportation.

The Dominican Republic is starting to renew visas for Haitians, but slowly. When you don't have a visa, you can't apply for some jobs, you can't open a bank account. If you get stopped by immigration, they're going to ask for your passport and you get deported. I'm telling you, the people that get deported, they don't have money. If you have money, they're going to take it from you and then drop you off on the road to Dajabón, the one that leads to Haiti. And you better know how to walk.

Though life in the Dominican Republic has been difficult, Jean remains endlessly inventive. He endures the disappointments and difficulties of unrealized plans, and continues to the next plan, always with the hope for the feeling of belonging to a place, and for his family to be in that place with him. But I worry, and he does, too, about a day when the hustle might not come through and I'll stop getting those messages at night, when Jean can't sleep: "Laura, I'm so worried…"

—*Laura Lampton Scott*

POSTSCRIPT

I'm sorry to say that MacDonald was shot three times last night trying to protect his mother from gang rape. They were staying in Baryè Boutèy, a neighborhood in Cap Haitien, bunking with friends. Gang members rushed into the house. MacDonald had gone out to buy something, and when he returned, he rushed in to save my wife and Geyonce. The machine gun went off *ta ta ta*, and the gang members ran out. Haiti is at war big-time and my family is still there!

I'm crying in pain and I don't know who to ask for help anymore. I failed my family in Haiti and I'm losing the battle for the ones here. I left them, and the rent has run out. I've not eaten. I've been living at my job. They let me sleep there, but that means I have to work extra hours without pay for living there. Nothing is free. I'm scared for my wife and kids to suffer more than what they are suffering now. My wife and my adopted daughter and my son are still in the cross fire.

My story's far from over.

DISPATCH: 1/26/24

I have no news from my family in Haiti.

The last I heard was they were looking for a hospital that would take MacDonald in. My wife and daughter have been hiding in a place for days now, and they have no food and little water. My wife doesn't have a phone, and I can't talk to her often.

No news since that day a week ago.

To make matters worse, I'm here in the DR with no place to stay and going from hotel to hotel. I sleep at my job on the weekdays, but on the weekends, I can't stay there, because the building is closed. The boss doesn't trust me to give me the keys.

I haven't seen my family that's here in the DR. I left them with the house we had rented. They are living off what's left of the deposit we paid. I want to visit, but I have nothing to bring them.

Lots of news, but there's nothing I can do. MacDonald is not dead, but he's in the hospital. They took him to King's Hospital in Port-au-Prince, one of the only hospitals open, and they wouldn't see him, because they assumed he was a gang member. My wife found my oldest son, David, who was visiting Port-au-Prince from the DR to do a big billboard job. David went to the police and filed a report about what happened, so they could prove to the hospital that MacDonald was a victim and not a gang member.

MacDonald got shot in the leg and hand and heart. There's a bullet next to his heart, and he needs surgery. David paid $1,600 for the metal setting for MacDonald's leg, and he'll get half back when they return it. We were lucky, because David had just made $2,500 for painting that billboard.

My wife and kids back there are in danger. I've been hiding out from all my problems, just smoking weed and drinking on the streets. Weekends are the worst because I can't sleep at my job. My kids here have been saying that I abandoned them.

MacDonald's leg is infected and they are asking us to leave the hospital because we can't pay. I lost my job. I wasn't able to work because of my living conditions. I'm giving up hope. Do you see how this all goes around and around?

I'm thinking about selling my phone. It's the only thing I have left.

I'm not stable on the streets, trying to find a place to lay my head. I've been walking all day and night. I'm feeling very sad and lonely and miss my family.

Annesamma finished her last high school class. She's seventeen. She's going to college now. It's free and she's very smart. She scored really high on the SAT and she speaks Spanish great.

That's one reason I want to stay alive. To see my kids grow.

ACKNOWLEDGMENTS

Jean, Peter, and Laura would like to thank Evan Lyon for his essential part in our early work together. We're lucky to have been the recipients of the lion-sized heart he lends to anything he's involved in. We'd also like to thank Yukiko Tominaga and Jeffrey Wolf for essential editing and transcription assistance, as well as Sarah Royalty Pinkerton for her early editorial guidance. Thanks to Chris Monks, a portion of this book was first published in *McSweeney's* online under the title "The Four Deportations of Jean Marseille." Gratitude to Caitlin Van Dusen for her exacting skill and patience with our loose use of the comma. Sunra Thompson and Annie Dills made this book look beautiful and we're thankful for their enthusiasm and style. And a huge thank-you to Amanda Uhle for her faith in Jean's story, and to Dave Eggers for his support of *Dispatches*. Thank you to our families for their support of our work on this book, especially to Jean's family for being so willing to share their lives.

ABOUT THE AUTHOR

JEAN MARSEILLE is a father, journalist, and call-center worker, with a background in many trades. He's worked with journalists from publications including *CNN*, *The New York Times*, *The Los Angeles Times*, and the *BBC*. He lives in the Dominican Republic with his family.

ABOUT THE EDITORS

PETER ORNER is a fiction and nonfiction writer and is the author of seven books, most recently a collection of essays called *Still No Word from You*. For the *Voice of Witness* series, he edited three volumes of oral history, including *Underground America: Narratives of Undocumented Lives*, *Hope Deferred: Narratives of Zimbabwean Lives*, and *Lavil: Life, Love, and Death in Port-au-Prince* (coedited with Evan Lyon and Laura Lampton Scott). He's chair of the English and Creative Writing Department at Dartmouth College and lives in Vermont.

LAURA LAMPTON SCOTT is an editor and writer. Her work has appeared in *Hobart*, *68to05*, *Michigan Quarterly Review*, and other publications. Laura is a MacDowell Colony fellow and teaches at Portland State University.

ABOUT THE *DISPATCHES* BOOK SERIES

Dispatches is a new series of powerful and compact nonfiction titles documenting the highs and lows of daily human endurance, as they happen. Edited by award-winning writers Peter Orner and Laura Lampton Scott, each book originates in short confidences recorded by individuals during borrowed moments. Set amid some of our most pressing contemporary predicaments, these invaluable books provide a vital firsthand look into lives rarely put to paper. This is the first book in the series.